THE COMPLETE SAXOPHONE PLAYER

BOOK 4

by Raphael Ravenscroft.

This book © Copyright 1988 & 1993 by Hal Leonard

Book designed by Sands Straker.
Cover designed by Pearce Marchbank.

ISBN: 978-0-7119-0890-1

Visit Hal Leonard Online at
www.halleonard.com

Contact us:
Hal Leonard
7777 West Bluemound Road
Milwaukee, WI 53213
Email: info@halleonard.com

In Europe, contact:
Hal Leonard Europe Limited
42 Wigmore Street
Marylebone, London, W1U 2RY
Email: info@halleonardeurope.com

In Australia, contact:
Hal Leonard Australia Pty. Ltd.
4 Lentara Court
Cheltenham, Victoria, 3192 Australia
Email: info@halleonard.com.au

Contents

About This Book

The fourth book in 'The Complete Saxophone Player' series will take the student to professional standard. Fingerings for the altissimo register are given, and microphone technique, overtones and section playing are explained.

The book contains an extensive guide to jazz soloing and improvisation, examining both the chordal approach and the use of upper and lower auxiliaries.

By learning to play popular songs and well known solos, the student quickly progresses to professional level. Although this course has been designed for home or classroom use, the clear instructions and diagrams make it particularly useful to students who do not have the benefit of regular tuition.

OK. Let's get professional.

Raphael Ravenscroft

Session 1: Glisses And Effects

Many different glisses and effects have been used in the next piece 'Baker Street'. So before playing this classic of the 1970's it will be a good idea to get to know at least some of them. One of the special features of the saxophone is its ability to allow the player to manipulate its sound, even after the note has been played (i.e. as long as you have air in your lungs you still have the facility to alter/bend/flatten/thicken/growl/vib/flutter). There is also a choice of techniques which you can use to 'approach' and play a note. Here are some of the options available:

Heavy Accent
Hold full value.

Heavy Accent
Hold less than full value.

Heavy Accent
Short as possible.

Staccato
Short – not heavy.

Legato Tongue
Hold full value.

The Shake
A variation of the tone upwards – much like a trill.

Lip trill
Similar to shake, but slower and with more lip control.

Wide Lip Trill
Same as above except slower and with wider interval.

The Flip
Sound note, raise pitch, drop into following note (done with lip on brass).

The Smear
Slide into note from below and reach correct pitch just before next note. Do not rob preceding note.

The Doit
Sound note then gliss upwards from one to five steps.

Du
False or muffled tone.

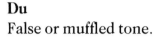

Wah
Full tone – not muffled.

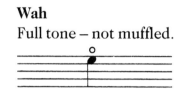

Short Gliss Up
Slide into note from below (usually one to three steps).

Long Gliss Up
Same as above except longer entrance.

Short Gliss Down
The reverse of the short gliss up.

Long Gliss Down
Same as long gliss up in reverse.

Note: No individual notes are heard when executing a gliss.

Short Lift
Enter note via chromatic or diatonic scale beginning about a third below.

Short Spill
Rapid diatonic or chromatic drop. The reverse of the short lift.

The Plop
A rapid slide down harmonic or diatonic scale before sounding note.

Long Lift
Same as above except longer entrance.

Long Spill
Same as above except longer exit.

Indefinite Sound
Deadened tone – indefinite pitch.

Baker Street
Words & Music by Gerry Rafferty

Note that the figure five relating to the groups of semiquavers in the penultimate bar signifies that these five notes should be played in the time of one beat.

Session 2: Chromatic Exercises And Whole Tone Scale Riffs

The interval between each note of a Chromatic Scale is invariably a semitone: the interval between each note of a Whole Tone scale is invariably a tone.

Regular slow and careful practice of these scale-riffs will assist you with:

1. Articulation
2. Intonation
3. Phrasing
4. Sight-reading. Note and phrase recognition.
5. Development of technical ability, correctly formed embouchure, and controlled diaphragmatic breathing.

Helpful advice:

Phrasing: I have written the scales (in Part 2 of this session) without phrasing marks, the addition of which I have left to the individual player.

Study the following examples:

Articulation:

Practise all the scales in Part 2 of this session with different types of articulation. Try to develop a precise, light, action of the tongue, taking care to maintain a relaxed embouchure and adequate air support.

Developing Your Technique

Always practise slowly, concentrate on evenness, while maintaining the same sound quality in both registers of the instrument.

Knowledge and practise of the following scale riffs will play an indispensable part in developing your technical control of the saxophone.

Session 2: (Part 2) Chromatic And Whole Tone Exercises

The following exercises are based on the whole tone and chromatic scales which we have already discussed. Be sure to include at least some of them in your daily practice routine.

Chromatic intervals

Chromatic intervals, which are excellent intonation studies, should be practised *very* slowly. After the intervals are well in tune, gradually increase the tempo. If there are rough spots in these exercises, they should be worked out separately until they do not hold up the tempo of the remainder of the progression.

Use several different articulations.

Session 3: Microphone Technique.
More Tips On Vibrato

Your vibrato needs to be slightly exaggerated on the stage/concert platform in order to make it sound effective to an audience seated some distance away. This same reduction in effect also occurs during the recording process. Compensating for this vibrato loss is part of the art of microphone technique. It is invariably gained by observation and experience (not to mention a certain amount of luck).

Watch out for the semi-quaver triplets in bars 6, 15, 22 and 42. Play them as you would quaver triplets, not forgetting they are to be played twice as fast. Concentrate on your vibrato and remember to make the vibrato waves slower on the lower notes, and a little faster and more urgent on the higher ones (second register).

This song was written to be played *slowly*. Attempting to perform it too quickly will (a) make it virtually impossible to play and (b) be of no practical benefit to your vibrato training.

This Masquerade
Words & Music by Leon Russell

Session 4: Group Playing Techniques

One of the most common faults in ensemble playing is the lack of attention which new players pay to the *duration* of the notes, especially those which are followed by a rest.

It is not always easy to accurately judge the duration of long notes, and giving long notes less time than they are worth is one of the most common (and irritating) faults found in novice reed and brass players. Solo playing allows some 'artistic licence' in note duration – section playing requires *exact* timing.

Here is a diagrammatic example of a dotted minim.

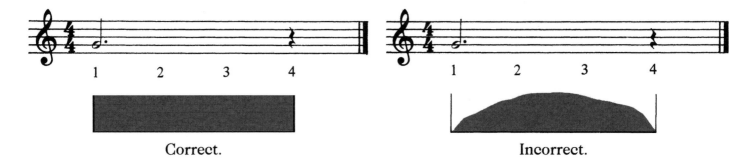

Correct.

Incorrect.

The dotted minim is held *until* the fourth beat.

Playing fast, short note phrases in a section also requires some care. It is very important to pay attention to legato, staccato and slur marks. A horn section should phrase as one man.

This next piece is a chance to practise a classic example of a hit record made up of saxophone section riffs. Get hold of a copy and listen to how the pro's 'do it'. If possible get together with fellow musicians and practise with your own section.

Pick Up The Pieces
By Roger Ball & Hamish Stuart

D.S. and Fade

Session 5: Still Crazy After All These Years

Well, after all the concentration which you have expended why not take some time out to enjoy this great ballad, composed and performed by Paul Simon. If you get a chance to listen to the original recording, note especially one of its outstanding features – the classic alto solo/end refrain played by the man himself, 'Mr David Sanborn'.

Still Crazy After All These Years
Words & Music by Paul Simon

Session 6: Repeat Bars And Time Signatures

Here are some examples of 'musical shorthand'.
N.B. This type of writing is not usually found in
song copies, but is very common in 'band parts'.

This sign **/** means that you repeat the preceding
group of notes. i.e.

is played:

This sign **%** means that you repeat the preceding
bar. i.e.

is played:

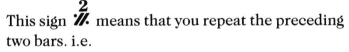

This sign **2 %** means that you repeat the preceding
two bars. i.e.

is played:

Four bar repeats 4/⫶ , and even eight bar repeats 8/⫶ may be encountered in your musical career, but a good arranger/copyist will write out those sections in full.

Some of you will have recognised the two bar repeated section as the opening riff from the Pink Floyd hit 'Money'. Before we finish this session, I want you to play through the melody of this famous song. It is one of the most demonstrative examples of a tune containing many different time signatures within what is a simple but effective melody.

Money
Words & Music by Roger Waters

FINE

Session 7: Super High Notes. Up Into The Altissimo Register.

The extension to the upper range of the saxophone has long been a controversial subject, largely due to the fact that no one saxophone is ever the same as another. Let me explain:

What Is the Harmonic Series?

You have probably realised already that every note you play on your saxophone is comprised not of one note, but of several. This natural phenomenon is known as the 'Harmonic Series'. Even though you do not hear these notes, as the principle notes, you can be sure that there are several harmonics present.

Looking at it another way, the main note i.e. the fundamental note, is the strongest of these several notes/tones, and is the pitch at which the note is heard. Therefore, each of the other notes/tones is called a 'harmonic' or 'overtone'.

Since all notes/tones above the normal saxophone range require the player to be able to manipulate the fundamental note/tone into its upper partials, before trying the actual harmonic fingerings it is essential to practise the following preliminary exercises. These exercises, employing only the first eight partials of the harmonic series will help you to:

1. Accustom your embouchure to this different type of note production.

2. Establish a firm aural foundation on which to build your already familiar instrument range of two octaves and a fifth. Remember that the addition of even a couple of notes to the range of the saxophone will contribute immeasurably to its scope and overall musical presentation.

Obtaining the Natural Overtones. Part 1: Harmonics

It will be necessary for you to change not only your embouchure, but also your air pressure and the way you deliver air to the mouthpiece, if you wish to bypass the fundamental note/tone and cause one of the harmonic overtones to be heard as the main pitch instead.

To do this you will need to strengthen your embouchure, forming a firmer circle (Book 1 p.17) and exposing a little more of the reed tip on the inside of your mouth by making a very slight forward movement of the jaw – *not* by inserting more of the mouthpiece into the mouth.

Your overall air pressure will need to be increased steadily as the higher harmonics are attempted – the equation being the higher the note/tone the smaller the amount of air (under greater pressure) used.

The following example of notes/tone is better
known as a 'harmonic series' and can be played/
practised on all the saxophone 'family'.

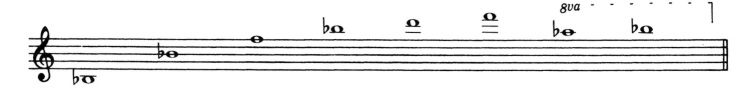

These high notes always require a little extra jaw
support to help keep them in tune. Don't forget
the following points:

1. Don't pinch the reed, it will not respond if it is
strangled.

2. Keep your embouchure as relaxed as possible
or the note will wobble.

3. Use more of your diaphragm than you would
normally do to support the high note and keep it
in tune.

Session 8: Fingering Diagrams
Altissimo Register

There is no one complete fingering diagram for the altissimo register, nor can there ever be one. There is not even one fingering in this range which can be called the 'correct' one.

It has taken me many years to compile the following fingerings, many of them have come from some of the world's top performers . . . David Sanborn . . . Mike Brecker . . . Junior Walker . . . Others are the result of many hours spent browsing through old downbeat articles,

past and present saxophone tutors and countless hours of experimenting with the seemingly endless flow of options. The first fingering which I have given for each note is the one which I prefer to use – but it may well not 'work' for you so I have included some alternatives.

At least some of these notes/tones should be included in your practice sessions. Add each new super note which you learn to your scales and patterns.

Fingering diagrams for the altissimo register:

N.B. For an explanation of the signs and symbols used in these diagrams refer to the chart in Book One of this course.

Octave key down on all notes.

All notes 8va. (octave up).

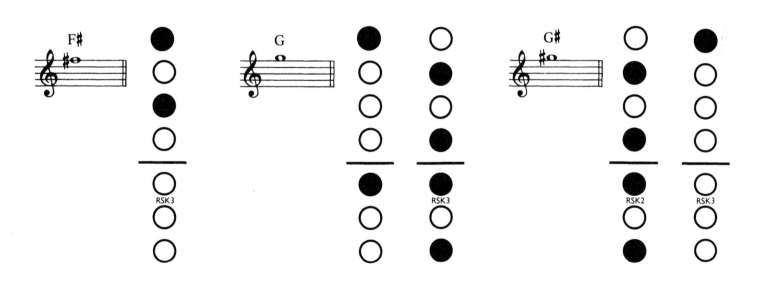

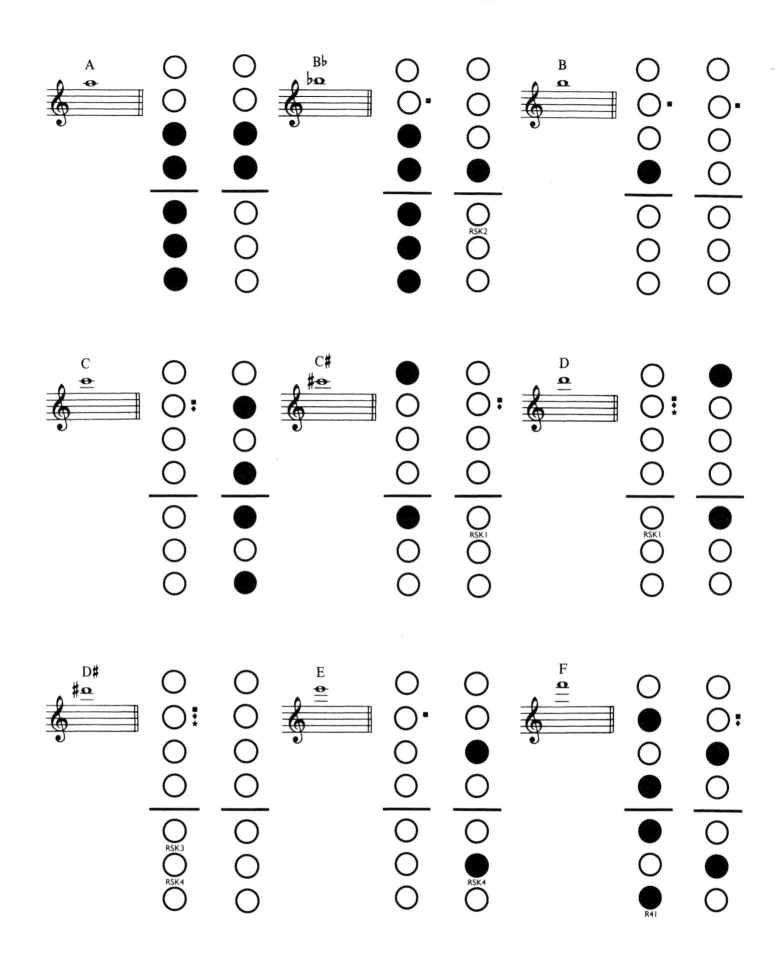

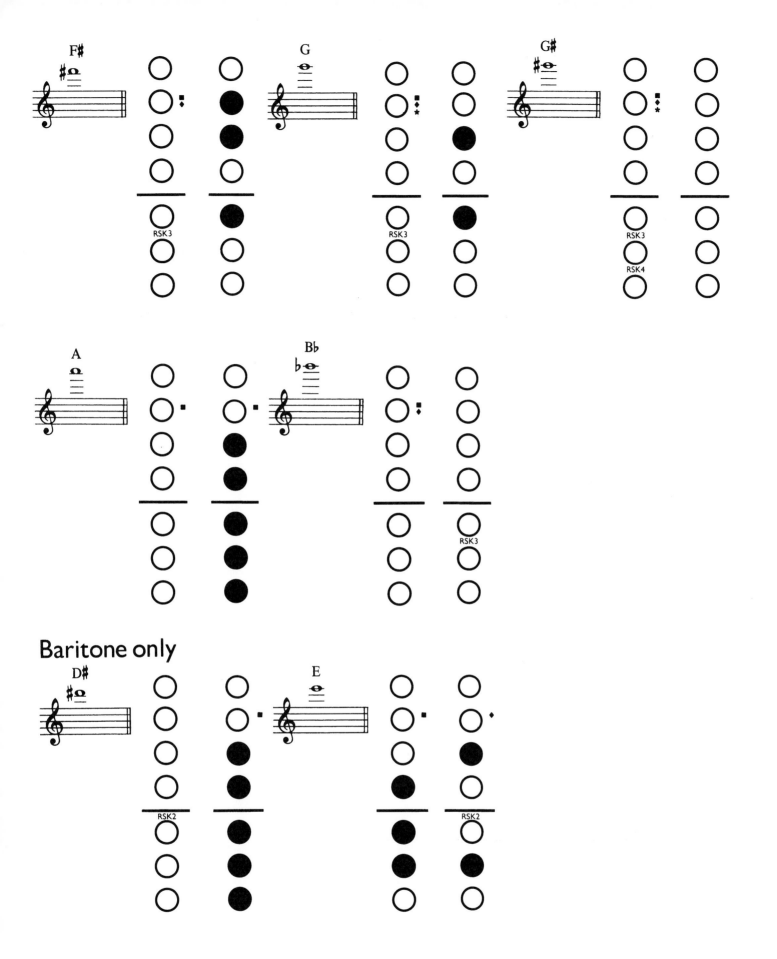

When you feel confident with this tune in the
register in which I've written it, try to learn a part
of it by heart. (*suggested sequences) Then
transpose these sections up an octave by *ear*.

Urgent
Words & Music by Mick Jones

If you are having difficulty in remembering both the tune and the fingerings, why not write part of it one octave higher than the music. You can then make notes on your score to show the alternative fingerings that work for you.

Session 9: The Importance of Imitation

If you are not entirely satisfied with your sound, the following exercises will not only help you to improve your overall tone but will also pinpoint the areas in which you need to improve.

Before you begin, listen to a recording of one of your favourite saxophone solos. Get the sound into your 'mind's ear' so that your embouchure muscles can start working towards creating a similar tone.

Practising long notes is one of the best ways to improve your sound tone. It helps to focus your attention on sound production and avoid the distraction of the intricate problems of reading, fingering, breathing etc.

Keep the octaves in tune with each other. Practise with D's and C's as well.

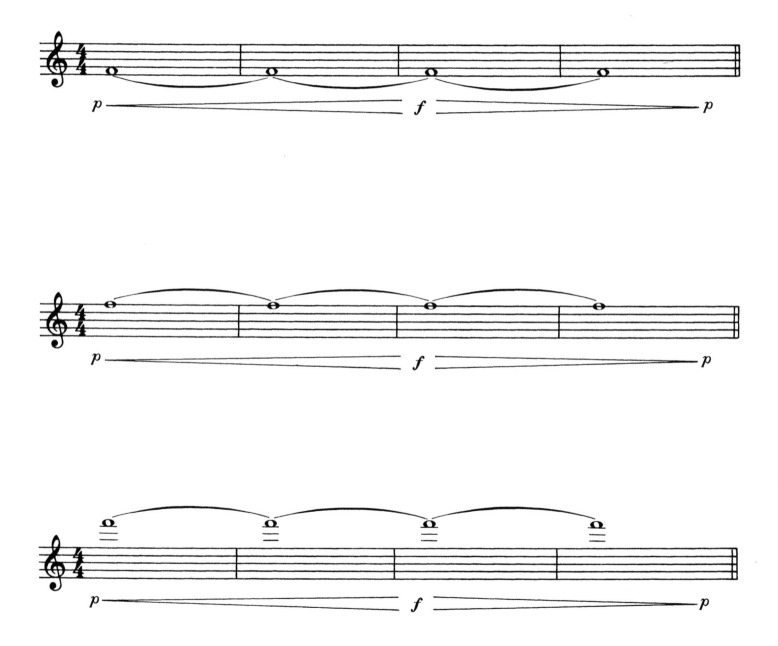

Another alternative to long note practise is the playing of slow melodies. The following ballad makes a perfect 'practice piece'.

He Ain't Heavy…He's My Brother

Words by Bob Russell Music by Bobby Scott

*Of course you can vary the tempo, in fact I
suggest that you do.*

Session 10: Developing Your Very Own Personal Tone (Part 2)

No two players sound exactly the same, the main reason being that we all have our own personal and highly individual qualities.

Even when playing the simplest melodies the largest single contribution you make is via your own personal tone. Of course, tonal characteristics are also influenced by your choice of instrument, the make and strength of your reed, type of mouthpiece, vibrato amount, type of vibrato and the volume at which you play. But although these factors modify your sound considerably, it remains a fact that you, and only you, determine the end result with the help of the many muscles in your jaw, cheeks, lips, throat, chest and diaphragm. Like an accent in your speech, your tone is largely acquired by imitating the sound of other players.

To develop your tone:

1. Choose your teacher wisely. Find one whose tone you admire.

2. Listen to your favourite players – attend rehearsals . . . go to live gigs . . .

3. Play along with recordings made by your favourite players.

4. Record your playing, and listen to the quality of your sound, especially in slow, simple melodies. Play these recordings to your teacher who will give you an honest assessment of your progress.

This next song is yet another slowish ballad. It is, in fact, not only an old standard, but a solid favourite amongst the jazz fraternity both young and old.

Ain't Misbehavin'
Words by Andy Razaf Music by Thomas Waller and Harry Brooks

Don't forget to use a little vibrato on the longer notes.

Session 11

The next piece is very interesting to play and will add yet another important tune to your repertoire. Together with 'The Pink Panther' and 'Baker Street' this is one of the most frequently requested saxophone solos.

Watch out for:

1. The new time signature 5/4. As the sign indicates, 5/4 comprises 5 crotchets (5 quarter notes) to the bar.

2. The dotted minims (eighth notes).

Playing hints
Study the first bar in depth. Analyse it, clap it, hum it, finger it without blowing. Then when you feel really confident play it, move on to the next bar and so on throughout the piece.

Take Five
By Paul Desmond

Session 12

The next tune is a very popular bossa nova made famous in the late 1950's by American tenor player Stan Getz and his quartet. Watch out for the unusual use of accidentals. For the most part they are used to bring notes back to their unaltered state, as opposed to their normal function of flattening or sharpening.

Look through the tune before playing and remember, for example, that the note C flat is B natural written in another form. The phrasing marks in this piece are very important. Practise the 5 bars below, paying particular attention to the staccato notes. These bars occur in the last 12 bars of the tune.

Desafinado

English lyrics by Jon Hendricks & Jessie Cavanaugh
Music by Antonio Carlos Jobim

Session 13

Here's another famous bossa nova, first recorded by Stan Getz in the early 1960's.

Note: I've used only four types of articulation:

— = play long.

∧ = play short.

• = play very short.

> = play normal accent.

I've left all other decisions regarding articulation and expression to the discretion of the individual player.

The Girl From Ipanema (Garota De Ipanema)
Music by Antonio Carlos Jobim

Session 14: An Introduction To Improvisation

Improvisation is an essential skill for all saxophone players. There are two main ways in which to approach the subject:

1. *The Analytical method* in which the player studies the music carefully before dissecting it into its many different parts, e.g. Rhythms, Chord Changes, Scale Patterns, Tempo . . .

2. *The Aural method* in which the player works mainly by 'ear', finding his way through the accompanying chord sequences by choosing notes which appeal to his own particular taste. Exponents of the aural method practise by playing along with tapes or records. Particularly useful for this are the specially produced tapes/records of a rhythm section playing a song accompaniment which allow you to provide your personal style of improvisation.

Most professional players use a combination of both methods, only by experimenting will you know which method is the one for you.

When musicians speak of a player having 'good ears', they usually mean that the person has realised the importance of analytical *listening*. 'Good ears' means having the ability to react to scales, chords, and intervals, either played by someone else or occurring in a player's own mind as an idea.

The basic tools of improvisation.
Improvising is not easy and will require some serious effort – don't be impatient, 'good ears' are developed over a lifetime of playing experience.

Singing and playing the following exercises will help the saxophone player to acquire the skill. Singing is very important as it helps to develop a sense of pitch.

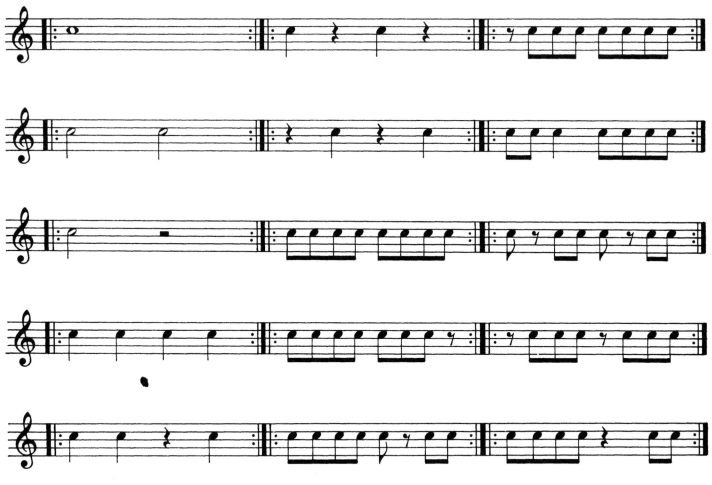

Session 15: Harmony; Intermediate Examples. Triads. Dominant 7th Chords. Seventh Chords

Harmony: Intermediate Examples

A knowledge of harmony enables the saxophone player to be creative and to use his musical skill and initiative to foster an even greater knowledge of music as a whole.

For this session, put your instrument back in its case – this is where concentrating on theory will pay dividends and will bring you even closer to becoming a 'complete' saxophonist.

Apart from its letter name, each note of the scale has a technical term.

The 1st note of the scale is known as –
The Tonic

The 2nd note of the scale is known as –
The Supertonic

The 3rd note of the scale is known as –
The Mediant

The 4th note of the scale is known as –
The Subdominant

The 5th note of the scale is known as –
The Dominant

The 6th note of the scale is known as –
The Submediant

The 7th note of the scale is known as –
The Leading Note

The 8th note of the scale is known as –
The Octave

Therefore in the key of C major:

C is the tonic
D is the supertonic
E is the mediant
F is the subdominant
G is the dominant
A is the submediant
B is the leading note
C is the octave (tonic)

Triads

Each note of a scale has its own triad (three note chord) of which it forms the root.
In the key of C major the triads are as follows:

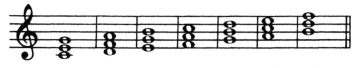

Tonic   Super-tonic   Mediant   Sub-dominant   Dominant   Sub-mediant   Leading-note

There are three major triads: Tonic, Subdominant and Dominant.

There are three minor triads: Supertonic, Mediant and Submediant.

There is one diminished triad: on the Leading note. It is called a diminished triad because the fifth is diminished and not perfect.

All chords can be inverted i.e. the lowest note (of the chord and) of any inversion can be raised an octave. Triads have only two inversions, the third inversion being the same as the root position an octave higher.

The tonic, subdominant and dominant chords of C major in their root position, first inversion and second inversion.

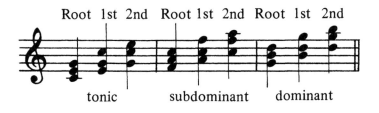

Root 1st 2nd   Root 1st 2nd   Root 1st 2nd

tonic   subdominant   dominant

Dominant 7th Chords

Before 'building' the dominant 7th chord in the key of Cmajor, examine the construction of the G triad in its root position. Notice that it is made up of a major third (G-B), and a minor third (B-D). To this triad we add another minor third (D-F). We have now constructed the chord of the dominant 7th.

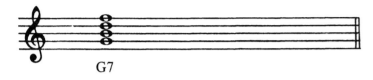

G7

This chord can also be inverted, and as a four note chord will in fact invert three times:

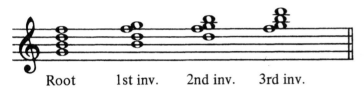

Root   1st inv.   2nd inv.   3rd inv.

Put another way: the term 7th applied to a chord means that the interval between the top note and bottom note of the chord in its root position is an interval of a 7th using the scale notes of its 'parent' key i.e. Cmajor.

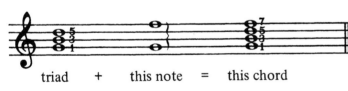

triad   +   this note   =   this chord

Seventh Chords

Resolving The Dominant 7th

When a seventh chord moves to the tonic chord it is commonly known as 'The Resolution of the Dominant Seventh'.

The following example shows how a note in one chord must proceed in a definite movement to a note in another chord. This note is said to have a fixed progression.

G7 – C   G7 – C   G7 – C   G7 – C

The 5th of the 7th chord may be omitted when the chord is in its root position, but in its inverted form all the notes of the chord must be present.

In general, the 5th note of a chord may be omitted in any position (except in 7th chords) but the *third of the chord . . . never.*

Here are all the inversions of the tonic, subdominant, dominant and dominant seventh chords in the key of C major.

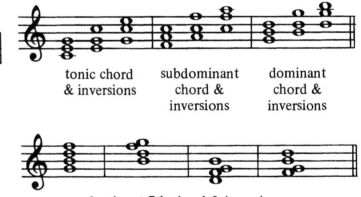

tonic chord   subdominant   dominant
& inversions   chord &   chord &
                    inversions   inversions

dominant 7th chord & inversions

Session 16

After all that music theory, the next song will
come as a 'breath of fresh air'. As always, read
through the music first and make a mental note of
all the important points e.g. time signature,
2nd time bars, repeat bars.

Ain't No Sunshine

Words & Music by Bill Withers

Session 17: Improvisation

Improvisation is creating your own personal melodic and harmonic interpretation of a melody. There are various ways of doing it. This session will deal with the analytical approach which requires:

1. The ability to recognise and use rhythm.

2. The technical skill to perform the improvisation on your instrument.

3. A basic knowledge of harmony and peripheral subjects.

In the following improvisation, based on the first two bars of 'Three Blind Mice', we use a harmonic device called an 'upper auxiliary'. This is a scale note above the principal note.

original melody

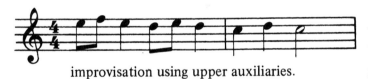

improvisation using upper auxiliaries.

From the C major scale the student can readily see the upper auxiliary of any given note in the key of C.

Don't forget that:
D is the upper auxiliary of C
F is the upper auxiliary of E
G is the upper auxiliary of F and so on.

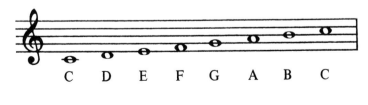

Our next step is to learn the function of the lower auxiliary which is a note a semitone below the principal note. It is usually sharpened.

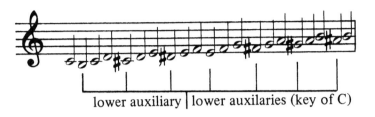

lower auxiliary | lower auxilaries (key of C)

Now let us look at a simple melody and see how upper and lower auxiliaries work together.

Remember this basic rule: the principal note is followed by the auxiliary which must always return to the principal note.

The Passing Note.
During the course of a melody two principal notes frequently follow each other by an interval of a third. This is where we need to use a passing note.

The passing note proceeding upwards.

✳ denote the passing note

The passing note proceeding downwards.

The next song, which was recorded by Roxy Music, is a perfect example of the use of auxiliaries and passing notes. Try to listen to the record and become familiar with the tune, then play along with it. The melody has been transcribed in its recorded key.

Avalon

Words & Music by Bryan Ferry

Session 18: Playing On Chords/
The Harmonic Approach

Now let us take a really simple tune and see what we can do with it by improvising.

We can see from the music that the first melody note is based on the chord of C, the second on the chord of G7 and the third also on C. So what does this tell us?

Firstly, that the notes built on the chord of C give us the notes C, E, G, to use in our improvising. With those built on the chord of G7 we have the notes G, B, D, F, at our disposal. They can be used in any order and with any rhythmic pattern.

An infinite number of variations can be based on this very simple melody. Here are some examples – practise them, then try working some out for yourself.

Chordal notes can be combined with auxiliaries and passing notes.

Improvisation

As you can see there is absolutely no restriction on how the notes in the various chords are employed. The only advice I can give the student at this point in *Book Four* is:
Keep It Simple!!!

N.B. All the improvisations in this session are based on the first two bars of 'Three Blind Mice'.

Here is an example of the clever use of auxiliaries,
and passing notes in a popular modern song.

With A Little Help From My Friends

Words & Music by John Lennon and Paul McCartney

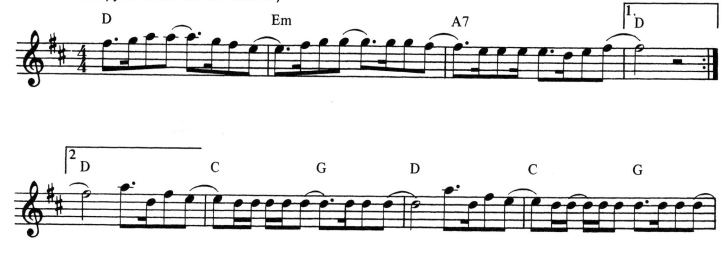

Session 19: Examples Of Improvisation

Try not to make the common mistake of playing
too many notes when you first begin to improvise.
Technique for technique's sake is not the answer.
Start simply, choosing your riffs with great care.
Play these examples slowly, gradually moving up
to the correct speed.

It may sound obvious, but try to *listen* to what
you play. Don't ever practise with your ears
'closed'.

Session 20: More On Improvisation

Here is a chance to examine the improvisational style of one of the 'giants' of modern jazz. I have transcribed from a recording by Miles Davis, part of a solo from 'Four' – one of his own compositions. Notice how Miles combines chordal improvisation with the use of upper and lower auxiliaries.

Play through this solo a few times and then try to add your own individual approach to the chord sequence.

Four

By Miles Davis

With moderate motion

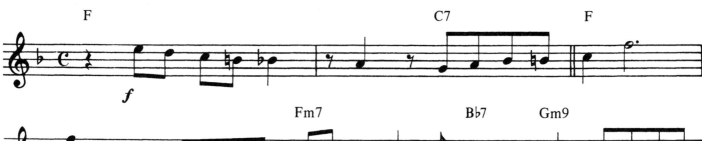

Session 21: Multiphonics

Multiphonics are 'simultaneously' produced notes (more than one note played at the same time) on a wind instrument. Their production will vary from player to player according to:

1. Make and age of your instrument.
2. Type of mouthpiece, type and strength of reed.
3. Embouchure control, breath control, etc.

The best way I have found to get them is by using a tight embouchure, and aiming for the top note of the chord. This is a list of the ones I use, with their approximate pitches:

1) The "Ugly Sound": Finger low C. Lift up the F key (first finger, right hand).

2) B♭ chord: Finger low B♭. Add the octave key.

3) B chord: Finger low B. Add the octave key.

4) C chord: Finger low C. Add the octave key.

5) D♭, D, and E♭ chords: Follow the same procedure as above.

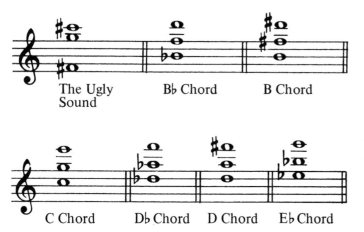

The Ugly Sound · B♭ Chord · B Chord

C Chord · D♭ Chord · D Chord · E♭ Chord

Other Tonal Effects, 'Growling'.

The technique of 'growling' is really quite simple. To make a 'growl': sing, or hum, while blowing a note in the normal way. Since the note you sing/hum will not be able to escape via your mouth (due to your mouthpiece blocking the air passage) it creates 'buzzy' vibrations in and around the oral cavity. These vibrations are then sent past the reed, causing a secondary vibration.

These oscillations end up by sounding just like a human growl and, used sparingly, are a useful effect for the modern saxophonist to include in his repertoire.

Note Bending

Bending a note colours the intonation and gives the saxophone a human, singing sound. You can start the note above or below its true pitch, or use your discretion to choose one of the infinite variations i.e. starting the note and then altering its pitch up or down.

To bend a note play it and *hold* it. Now release the pressure of the lower teeth and then return to your normal embouchure.

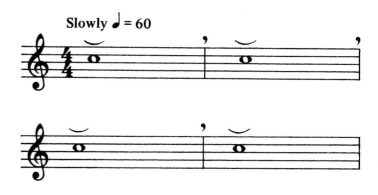

Session 22: Solo Breaks And Phrasing

The ability to create 'fills' and short solo breaks which complement a vocal line is not an easily acquired skill. Here are some points to remember: Be as clear and precise as you can, don't hesitate, there's never enough time. If the song has lyrics listen to them, feel the mood of the song and try to play within the confines of the style in which the tune was composed.
Don't play too much.

The following piece shows both melody and saxophone solo.

Year Of The Cat
Words & Music by Al Stewart and Peter Wood

The next song was a hit for The Crusaders who feature four of the finest jazzers you'll find.

Concentrate on the rhythmic phrasing.

Street Life
Words by Will Jennings Music by Joe Sample

A Few Final Words

Here you are, you made it! Congratulations. There are many people who pick up a musical instrument and promise themselves that they will learn to play, but few have the patience and willpower to come this far.

The options for further study are limitless, and it is up to you to continue to build on the solid foundations you now have. Your imagination is your only limitation and whatever it is you choose to do with your newly acquired skill, never forget that above all else, 'music should always be fun'.

As a last word of advice, don't forget to watch out for new developments. Try out new models of saxophones, reeds, mouthpieces, etc. Listen to the exciting exponents of the saxophone, get their records and don't forget if you want really up-to-date information on what's new, check out your local music store for instruments, music books, and sheet music.

Good Luck!